The Great Big Boat

by Sylvia Root Tester

illustrated by Robert Masheris

THE CHILD'S WORLD

ELGIN, ILLINOIS 60120

Library of Congress Cataloging in Publication Data

Tester, Sylvia Root.
   The great big boat.

   (Bible story books)
   SUMMARY: Brief text retells the story of Noah
and the flood.
   1. Noah's ark—Juvenile literature. 2. Bible
stories, English—O.T.   Genesis VI, 5-IX, 17.
[1. Noah's ark. 2. Bible stories—O.T.]
I. Masheris, Robert. II. Title. III. Series.
BS658.T47   222'.11'09505   79-12176
ISBN 0-89565-087-8

Distributed by Standard Publishing, 8121 Hamilton Avenue,
Cincinnati, Ohio 45231.

The Great Big Boat

The Biblical account of this story
is found in *Genesis 6:8—9:17*.

Noah was a friend of God.

"Noah," God said, "build a boat.
Make it big, a great big boat.
Soon there will be a flood,
a flood over the whole, wide world.
That flood will destroy
every living thing
that is not on My boat."

Noah was a friend of God.
So Noah built the boat.
He built it just as God wanted.
He built it wide
and very strong.
He built it tall.
He built it long.

"Noah," God said,
"bring all the animals
into the boat.
Bring two of every kind."

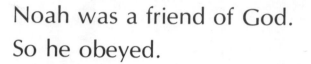

Noah was a friend of God.
So he obeyed.

Animals came, two by two,
from everywhere,
from all over the world,
to enter the great big boat.
Animals came, two by two—
cats, dogs,
antelopes, and zebras...

tigers, lions,
polar bears, and cougars.

Animals came, two by two,
elephants, beavers,
horses, and wolves…

15

giraffes, kangaroos,
koala bears, and gazelles.

Animals came, two by two,
gorillas and snakes
and many, many more.
Birds came flying
to the great big boat.
From everywhere,
from all over the world,
the great birds flew.

"Noah," God said, "bring your family
into the boat.
Soon the rain will begin."

Noah was a friend of God.
So he obeyed.
The rains came down,
poured and poured,
and water came up from below.

Soon the great big boat was floating,
floating and rocking, to and fro.
It rained and rained,
it poured and poured,
and then it rained some more.
For forty days and forty nights,
the rain came pouring down.

But Noah and his family
and all of the animals
were safe in their great big boat.
For Noah was a friend of God.

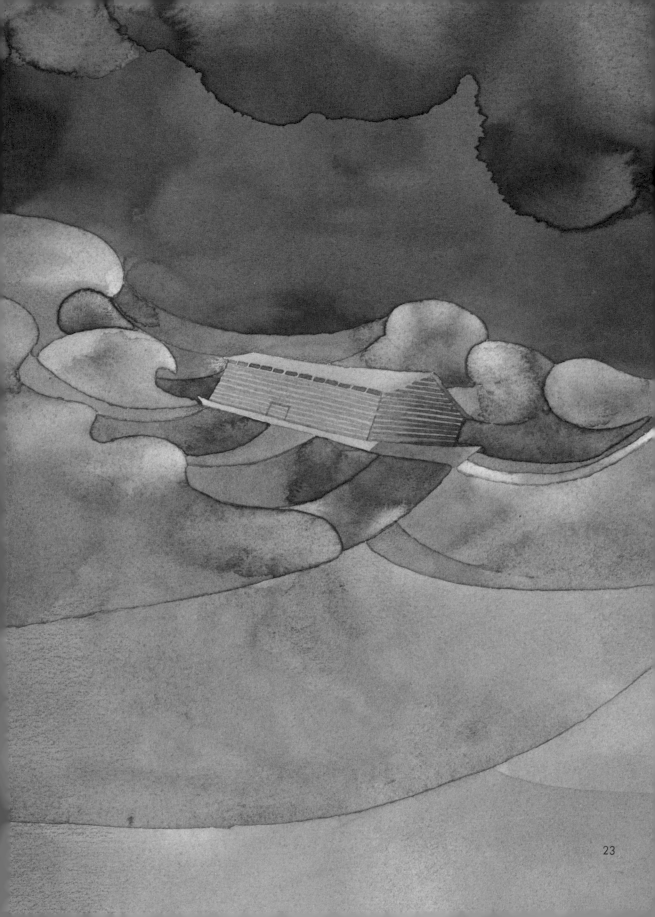

Finally, finally, the long rain stopped.
The sun shone bright and warm.
Noah looked out of his window.
Everywhere he looked,
there was water, only water.

Slowly, slowly, the water went down,
till the great big boat
landed on a high mountain.

Slowly, slowly, the water went down,
till, finally, it was safe.
Noah and his family
and all of the animals
walked out of the great big boat.

Noah was a friend of God.
"Thank You, God," he said,
"for saving us from the flood."

"There won't be a flood like this,"
God said, "not like this,
not ever again.
Look, Noah, look in the sky."

Noah looked up and saw...

a rainbow!

"The rainbow is My promise,"
God said.
"Never again a flood like this."